# FOLENS
# R.E.

# THINKING ABOUT RELIGION

## PETER CURTIS

# Thinking About Religion.

## Author's note

A part of the task of school Religious Education is to familiarise children with the principal beliefs and practices of the world's major faiths. Another part is to encourage them in their own thinking about the questions religions ask and the human experiences that give rise to those questions. Important to both of these concerns, however, is the requirement that children understand what a religion is and what it means to hold a religious faith. It is important, too, that they explore their own attitudes towards religion and the issues with which religion deals. It is to these particular objectives that **Thinking About Religion** addresses itself.

**Thinking About Religion** does not attempt to provide a comprehensive survey of the major world religions. It asks children to think about religion in general rather than religions in particular. By using it, children will certainly gain considerable knowledge about the world's major faiths, but, more importantly, they should gain an understanding of what it means to hold a religious faith whether they themselves hold one or not.

## Publisher's note

**Thinking About Religion** is one of a series of three textbooks written for school pupils and designed to stimulate their interest in the world of religion and the questions religions ask. The other two books in the series are entitled **Thinking About Living** and **Thinking Things Through**. Each book has a companion volume of photocopiable material.

ISBN 1 852760958

First published 1990 by Folens Limited, Dunstable and Dublin.

Folens Limited, Albert House, Apex Business Centre, Boscombe Road, Dunstable LU5 4RL, United Kingdom.
Printed in Singapore by Craft Print.

# Contents

# 1. What's it all about?

At the beginning of a book it's helpful to be told what it's about. That's what this unit tries to do.

Let me begin by explaining quite simply that this book is all about 'religion'. I wonder how you react to that. Let's find out straight away. Get a piece of paper and write three words that sum up your reaction. Then do Core Activity 1.

I wonder what thoughts came into your mind as soon as I mentioned the word 'religion'. Being sent to Sunday School years ago and perhaps wishing you could be doing something else instead? Long and not very interesting talks by a vicar? Arabic classes that you found difficult? Large, cold buildings? Having to dress up in clothes you didn't feel comfortable in? Elderly people, a bit old fashioned? Or perhaps it was something more positive. Being with friends? A church youth club? Doing things as a family? The glow of Sabbath candles or of the arti lamp? Celebrations at the end of Ramadan?

Spend just 3 or 4 minutes talking to a friend about what the word 'religion' brings immediately into your mind and write down some of the ideas. Then compare them with those of other pupils in your class.

*Learning Arabic isn't easy. Why do Muslims think it so important?*

*What is this building for?*

There are many religions in the world. You may know the names of some. See how many you can list. Alongside the religions of the world there are other beliefs that many people hold. You may have heard, for example, of Marxism or Humanism. This book will not attempt to tell you all you could know about any of these religions or other types of belief. There are lots of good books that can help you with that. Indeed, a very good thing to do is to look to see what books about religions are available in your school or local library because often I shall be asking you to go and find out about religions for yourself. What this book will help you to do is to understand better what a religion is, why many people hold religious beliefs, and why those beliefs are so important to the people who hold them.

Let's get one thing straight at the start. What you believe is your business. This book is not going to try to make you more (or less) religious. It's certainly not going to try to convert you to one particular religion. What it is going to try to do is to help you understand religion (and therefore religious people) better.

*Sabbath candles in a Jewish home evoke a very special feeling.*

EXTENSION ACTIVITIES

4 Visit your school library or a local public library and find the titles and authors of TWO books which describe a number of religions and ONE book which describes each of the following religions:

Buddhism, Christianity, Hinduism, Islam, Judaism, Sikhism

Try to find books that you think you could read and understand because you will need to go back to these books later on.

5 In a good dictionary look up the meanings of the following words:

belief, creed, faith, religion, worship

6 Compose a sentence that uses three of the words you've just looked up.

*The warmth of the arti lamp symbolises the blessing of God.*

## CORE ACTIVITIES

1 Make a collection of all the words your class thought of when told this book was about religion. Divide them into positive and negative reactions. Which were the more common?

2 Try to decide why you reacted as you did. Write just two or three sentences explaining your reasons.

3 Talk to somebody whose reaction was quite different from yours. Explain to each other why you reacted as you did. Can you understand the other person's point of view?

# 2. Are you religious?

I wonder whether you have ever asked yourself that question. This unit will make sure that you have! It will also explore what the question means.

**A**

*Is this singing religious? How would you decide?*

**C**

*Is this woman religious? How would you decide?*

**B**

*What's happening here? Why is the reading of this book treated differently?*

**D**

*What makes this a religious activity?*

Well, are you religious? There's no need to tell anybody else your answer, but do decide what your immediate answer to that question is. Then do Core Activity 1.

Of course, how you answered that question depends not only on what sort of a person you are but on what you understand the word 'religious' to mean. How could you tell if somebody was religious? Some questions you might ask are listed in **E**. In pairs or small groups, think about each in turn and decide whether the question would be a helpful one. Think of some good questions of your own.

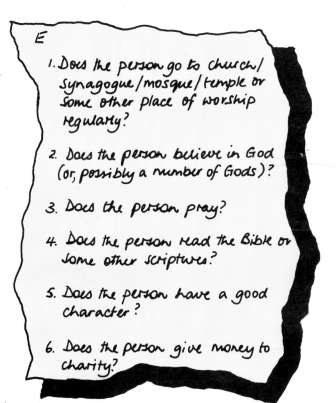

E

1. Does the person go to church/synagogue/mosque/temple or some other place of worship regularly?

2. Does the person believe in God (or, possibly a number of Gods)?

3. Does the person pray?

4. Does the person read the Bible or some other scriptures?

5. Does the person have a good character?

6. Does the person give money to charity?

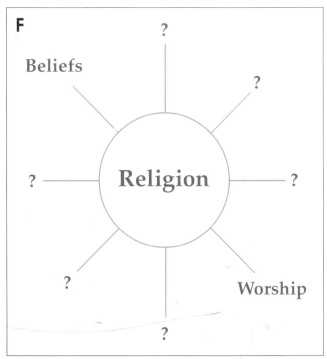

F

Beliefs

Religion

Worship

*The 'ingredients' of religion.*

Now, still in your pairs or groups, try to complete this sentence:

*For a person to be religious he or she must ...*

Compare your sentence with those of others in the class. As a class, which do you feel is the best sentence? Take a vote on it. Perhaps you can produce a better sentence still by combining the ideas of a number of groups.

## CORE ACTIVITIES

1 What made you decide as you did about whether you were religious or not? What do you do or not do, believe or not believe, that made you answer as you did?

2 Try your list of questions on two people that you know. Try to include one adult. See if they think your questions are good ones. (Maybe they can suggest some others.) From the answers they gave, would you describe these people as 'religious'? Would they agree with you?

3 Make a list of things you normally associate with somebody who is religious. (Be careful! Don't put specific things like 'going to church'. Muslims and Jews, for example, don't go to church.)

### EXTENSION ACTIVITIES

4 Visit or invite into your classroom somebody who would be happy to be described as 'religious'. Talk to that person about his or her religion. How well does that person fit the 'model' you came up with when you did Core Activity 3?

5 Produce a diagram to show what you think a religion should contain. Put the word 'religion' in the middle and arrows going out to the things (like beliefs) that are important parts of religions.

# 3. Does religion matter?

That's a pretty big question! In this unit we will start to answer it and one thing we must do is sort out what the question actually means.

However much or little you may have thought about religion, I hope you wouldn't try to give a 'yes' or 'no' answer to that question.

That's because the question is really incomplete as it stands. It's a bit like the question 'Is six bigger?' The question doesn't make sense. We have to ask 'Bigger than what?' It's the same with the question 'Does religion matter?' We have to ask 'Matter to whom?'

The sort of question we should ask is 'Does religion matter to the majority of people in this country?' or 'Does religion matter to my next door neighbour?' or 'Does religion matter to me?' When we ask a question like that it's possible to set about trying to answer it.

In Britain today there are not just thousands, but literally millions of people who belong to one religion or another. The majority of them are Christians.

*This matters to most Christians. Why?*

*Bowing symbolises respect for someone or something important.*

Christianity has been the main religion in this country for many centuries and its followers may belong to any one of a number of different parts of the Christian church. They may be Roman Catholics, Anglicans, Methodists, Baptists, or Pentecostalists, for example. In addition to a great many Christians, Britain has quite large numbers of Muslims, Hindus, Sikhs and Jews and smaller numbers of Buddhists and representatives of other religions.

In other countries, of course, the situation is reversed. In India, for example, Hindus form the majority. In Iran the majority are Muslims; in Burma, Buddhists. To a large extent, then, the religion to which you belong - if you belong to one at all - will depend upon the country in which you are born and the religion to which your parents belong. Most parents try to bring their children up into their own religious beliefs.

Though quite a number of people become committed to a religion they weren't born into, or lose their interest in the religion they were brought up in, not many change from one religion to another.

*Washing the image of the Hindu God, Siva. What might the washing signify?*

*Reading the scriptures matters to Sikhs.*

There can be no doubt at all that to millions and millions of people in this world religion does matter. It matters enough for them to take part regularly in religious activities. It matters enough for them to try to live their lives in accordance with their beliefs.

To some people religion has mattered enough to die for. There are many stories of religious martyrs. Can you think of any? To some it has mattered enough to kill for. Many persecutions have taken place in the name of religion. These may be exceptions, true, but to countless people religion has been and remains an extremely important part of their lives.

Look at the people in the pictures in this unit. They are all engaged in some form of religious activity. Look carefully at each picture and then try Core Activities 1 and 2.

You can ask the question 'Does religion matter?' not just about individual people but about whole countries. In this country, for example, there is a 'state religion', the Church of England, of which the Queen is the head. Much of the life of this country is affected by that religion. Many state ceremonies, like royal weddings or coronations, are religious ceremonies. Many of the laws of this country are based originally on Christian ideas. In addition, there are laws which protect the rights of people to hold whatever religious beliefs they wish. There are laws affecting what can and what cannot take place on a Sunday.

*Why does the seeking of peace matter?*

There is also a law in this country that says that school pupils should have a daily act of worship in school and should have religious education as a part of their school lessons. In so far as religion affects the whole of our country religion matters to all of us whether we are actively involved in it or not.

*Does religion matter to them?*

# CORE ACTIVITIES

1 Say which religion is represented by each picture in this unit. What are the clues that help you tell?

2 Using both your knowledge and your imagination, describe in as much detail as you can what is happening in each picture in this unit.
In what ways does religion matter to the people who are shown?

3 List any ways you can think of in which religion affects your life now. If you can't get started think about when school holidays come and why.

4 In small groups discuss the question whether religion matters to you.

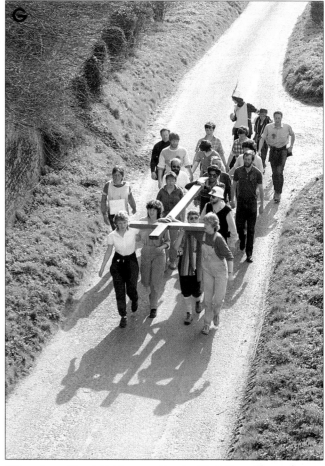

So, in addition to the people who belong to a religion, there are many people who take no part in religious activities and who would probably not describe themselves as 'religious' but whose lives are affected by religion in one way or another. To them religion matters, but in a different sort of way.

*Why does Good Friday matter to Christians?*

*Why was this building constructed?*

5 Watch the TV news regularly for a week. List any items that have something to do with religion. Does religion often make the news?

6 On a map of your area, mark any churches or other places of worship. Can you think of any other type of religious activity that goes on in your area?

7 Find out all you can about this country's laws relating to Sunday. For example, what can you or can't you buy and sell on a Sunday?

8 Why do so many people who do not go to church want their children baptised or want a church wedding?

# 4. Asking religious questions.

In the last unit we saw that there is a sense in which religion matters both to people who are religious and to those who are not. Religion can affect their lives in a variety of ways. But there's another way of understanding the question 'Does religion matter?' We could ask instead 'Does religion ask important questions?' Does it matter in that sense?

Have you ever wondered why religions exist? There must be a reason! As we have already said, there are many religions today and, as far as we know, there always have been religious beliefs and practices as long as the human race has existed. Anthropologists tell us that even the most ancient of human beings asked religious questions and expressed their answers to those questions in the form of religious beliefs and practices. It would seem that there is something about the human species that inevitably ends up asking religious questions!

*What, if anything, lies beyond death?*

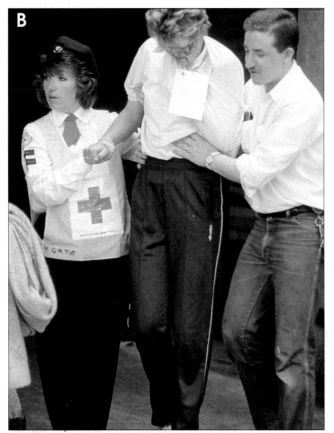

*Can you make sense of such suffering?*

It's the word 'Questions' that gives us a clue to at least one of the reasons for religion's existence. Religions don't exist because somebody clever makes them up. They exist because they seem to provide answers to some of the questions human beings find themselves asking about the lives they live and the world they live in. As we think about our lives we find ourselves asking some very deep questions. It is these questions that often lie at the root of religious beliefs.

It may sound rather morbid, but let's start with death. One of the most basic of human experiences is the experience of death. The members of an ancient tribe will have seen their members grow old and eventually die. In our modern world it is just the same. Death is one of very few things that happens to everybody. Inevitably people ask questions about death like those in **C**.

C

Why do we have to die?

Is death the end or is there something after death?

Do we have one life on this earth or many?

Is there somewhere where we go after death?

If so, where and what is it like?

Do people go to different places?

If so, who or what decides where each person goes?

D

*The Universe - accident or design?*

Let's take another example. All of us are aware of the world around us. Some people may understand it better than others. Scientists can tell us many marvellous things about it. But even if we are not particularly clever we can all enjoy its beauty, marvel at its incredible complexity and variety and wonder how it came into existence. Similarly, when we gaze up into the skies at night and see thousands of stars, we find ourselves asking all sorts of questions like those in **H**.

There are many other questions, but these will do as examples. There are, of course, many people who are interested in the answers to these questions but who do not follow any particular religion. Perhaps they would give answers to these questions which are different from those that religions have given. What we have to decide is whether questions such as those about death and the purpose of creation matter. If they do, then the answers that religions offer should be worth thinking about. If the questions matter, then religion matters because it suggests answers to these questions. If they don't, then maybe religion doesn't matter either. Only you can give your honest opinion as to whether such questions are important or not.

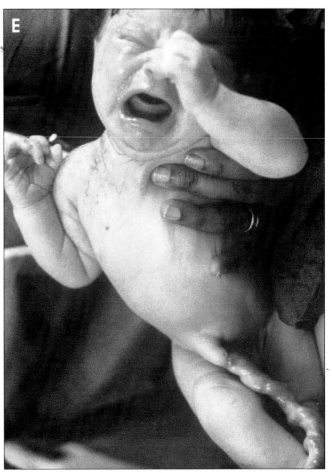

*Is there a purpose to life?*

*Death - the ultimate mystery?*

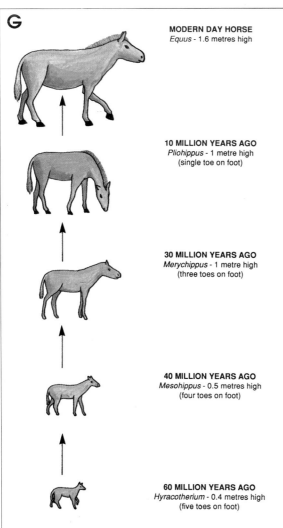

**G**

MODERN DAY HORSE
*Equus* - 1.6 metres high

10 MILLION YEARS AGO
*Pliohippus* - 1 metre high
(single toe on foot)

30 MILLION YEARS AGO
*Merychippus* - 1 metre high
(three toes on foot)

40 MILLION YEARS AGO
*Mesohippus* - 0.5 metres high
(four toes on foot)

60 MILLION YEARS AGO
*Hyracotherium* - 0.4 metres high
(five toes on foot)

*An adequate explanation?*

**H**

How did the universe come into existence?
Is there some purpose to it all?
Is there some purpose in us being here?
Why should there be millions of people standing on a huge lump of rock spinning in space?
Were we created for a reason?
Or is the whole of creation meaningless and purposeless?

If you think about it, you will quickly see that questions like those in **C** and **H** are just the sort that religions try to answer. Religious thinking arises straight out of the basic human experiences of death and of wondering about the world around us. The more you think about the questions religions explore - like why people suffer and how we should behave - the more you will see this to be true. Our experiences lead to some very deep and difficult questions. The religious beliefs that people hold often contain their answers to just those questions.

## EXTENSION ACTIVITIES

4 Ancient peoples often told stories that suggested answers to basic religious questions. Make up a story of your own that might explain one of the following:
  i Why people often quarrel with each other.
  ii Why human beings are different from each other.
  iii Why human beings are different from other creatures.

5 Choose one of the following and suggest the questions that might arise from it:
  i a disastrous earthquake
  ii the fact that there is life on earth
  iii evolution (look at **G**)
  iv the fact that there are many different religions.

## CORE ACTIVITIES

1 What answers would you give to the questions about death that were asked in this unit? Talk about this in pairs or think about it on your own if you would prefer. (Incidentally, the answer 'I honestly don't know' is a perfectly acceptable answer. There are many adults who would have to give that answer if they were asked.)

2 Here are two more questions that lie at the heart of religious thinking. Select one of them and suggest what experiences might cause people to ask that question.
  i How should one human being treat another?
  ii Does God exist?

3 Try to think of two more questions that religions grapple with. Do you have your own answers to those questions? If so, what are they?

# 5. The question of God.

Perhaps the most obvious of all religious questions is 'Does God exist?'. You will not get an answer to that question in this unit, but you will begin to explore some of the reasons why many people believe in God.

In almost every religion you will find belief in at least one God or Goddess and perhaps in many. That is true of religions today and it was true in the past. You may have heard the names of some of the Gods in which the ancient Romans and Greeks believed - names like Zeus, Mercury, Mars, Jupiter, Apollo, and Venus. Or you may have heard of Norse Gods like Thor and Odin. Today most of the major world religions hold that there is one God only. One of the essential parts of the beliefs of Muslims, for example is that there is one God, Allah - 'Allah' being the Arabic word for 'God' - and that worship should be given to Him alone. Sikhs, too, believe in one God. They sometimes speak of Him as 'Waheguru' which might be translated 'Wonderful Lord'.

*Belief in Gods stretches across the centuries.*

*Describe this artist's portrayal of God.*

Christians and Jews also believe that there is one God. In the Jewish Bible (which, incidentally, is the same collection of scriptures as Christians call the 'Old Testament') the name of God is written as four Hebrew letters which correspond to YHWH in English. But when Jews are reading the scriptures they will not pronounce this name. Instead they will say either 'Adonai' (which means 'My Lord') or 'Hashem' (which means 'the Name'). This is done because the name of God is thought too holy to pronounce. In Christianity God is not given a particular name but He is often spoken of as 'Heavenly Father' because Christians believe that this is a helpful way to think of God.

Hinduism is a little more complicated. If you study Hinduism you will hear the names of many Gods and Goddesses. You will hear of Vishnu, Siva and Brahma in particular, but also of Hanuman, Ganesha, Sarasvati, Krishna, Lakshmi, Kali and many others. In a sense, then, Hinduism has lots of Gods, but many Hindus would say that all these Gods are really aspects of the one true God.

*The Hindu deities, Radha and Krishna. Why are they dressed as they are?*

*The Hindu Goddess, Sarasvati.*

A question we have to ask is 'Why do so many people believe in one or more Gods?'. It would hardly make sense to believe in God for no reason. This is a difficult question, of course, but we can suggest some answers that might be true for at least some people.

Some people believe in God because they were brought up to do so when they were young. Perhaps their parents taught them when they were very young and so they have always believed. Many, of course, will, as adults, have come to accept for themselves what their parents taught them as children.

In the past and to some extent, no doubt, still today people have believed in God or Gods because that helped them explain things that otherwise seemed a mystery. When confronted by things they didn't understand, like violent storms or earthquakes for example, ancient peoples often turned to the idea of Gods to help them understand what had happened. Of course, the more that people came to understand their world the less need they had to explain things in this way, but there are people today who would say that they can make better sense of the world in which they live if they believe in God than they could if they didn't. Belief in God helps them explain some of the world's mysteries.

*This can still evoke awe and wonder.*

There have been people who have actually tried to prove that God exists. One proof that was attempted was to say that since everything that exists must have a cause, there must be something that was the very first cause of all. That first 'Cause', it was said, was God. Most people today, however, would agree that proof is impossible and that belief in God is a matter of faith.

## CORE ACTIVITIES

1 Find out the origins and meanings of the names of the days of the week and months of the year (look at **F**).

2 Look up the meaning of the following words in a good dictionary:
   i    atheism
   ii   henotheism
   iii  monotheism
   iv   polytheism

3 As a class, try to speak to at least ten people who believe in God. Find out why they believe. How similar are their reasons?

F

| Day/Month | Origin/Meaning |
|-----------|----------------|
| Sunday | the day of the sun |
| Monday | |
| Tuesday | |
| Wednesday | the day of the God Woden |
| January | from the Roman God, Janus |
| February | |
| March | from Mars, the Roman God of war |
| April | |

Some people believe in God because they claim to have had some direct experience of Him. Something has happened in their lives which they can explain in no way other than as an experience of God. This could be said of great figures from the past who became the founders of new religions - people like the Prophet Muhammad who believed that God was sending through him a series of revelations for the Arab people, revelations which were later written down in the form of the Muslims' holy book, the Qur'an. Another example is Guru Nanak, the founder of the Sikh religion, whose experiences of God led him to write hymns of praise to God which now form part of the Sikhs' scriptures, the Guru Granth Sahib. But it is true also of less famous people. Somebody, for example, who has felt 'called' to be a priest or minister would say that it was God who called him or her.

*Guru Nanak, founder of Sikhism.*

*What does this tell us about the Christian understanding of God?*

EXTENSION ACTIVITIES

4 Divide your class into 4 groups and let each group do some research about one of the following:
   i   Greek Gods
   ii  Norse Gods
   iii Egyptian Gods
   iv  Roman Gods

5 Find out what you can about the life of either the Prophet Muhammad or Guru Nanak.

6 Whatever your own personal beliefs may be, consider what evidence would be necessary to make you believe in God. What evidence would be necessary to make you believe that God does not exist?

# 6. What is God like?

People who believe in a God inevitably want to know what that God is like. This unit explores some of the answers that have been given to that question.

Since we have already said that we cannot prove that God exists perhaps we should phrase the question at the head of this unit differently. We should ask instead 'What do people believe God to be like?'. To answer that question we can look at two main things - what they say about God and how they portray God in various types of art. Let's look first at three examples of things that are said.

**B**

*Praise be to Allah, Lord of the worlds,*
*The compassionate and merciful,*
*Ruler on the Day of Judgement!*
*You alone we worship; you alone we ask for help.*
*Show us the straight path,*
*The path of those whom you have favoured,*
*Not the path of those who earn your anger*
*Or of those who go astray.*

**B** comes from Islam. This is the opening Sura (chapter) of the Qur'an. It is frequently recited by Muslims as a part of their prayers. Again, what does it tell us about the way Muslims think of God?

**A**

*There is one God,*
*Eternal Truth is His name.*
*He is the maker of all things*
*and He dwells in all things.*
*He fears nothing and He hates nothing.*
*He is immortal, unborn and self-existent.*
*He has been made known to men*
*by the grace of the guru.*

**A** comes from the Sikh religion. It is called the 'Mool Mantra'. Many Sikhs will say these words each day, first thing in the morning. Can you say in your own words the most important things this prayer tells us about the way Sikhs think of God?

*The Hindu Goddess, Mattaji, consort of Siva.*

**D** comes from Christianity. This is the most famous of all Christian prayers. It is called the 'Lord's Prayer' because Christians believe that Jesus taught it to his disciples as a model of how to pray. What does it tell us about the way Christians think of God?

D

Our Father in heaven, may your name be kept sacred.
May your kingdom come.
May your will be done on earth as it is in heaven.
Give us today our daily bread.
Forgive us what we have done wrong As we forgive those who have done wrong to us.
Do not lead us into temptation, but deliver us from evil.
For yours are the kingdom, the power and the glory.
Now and for ever.

*Why the crown? And why no pain?*

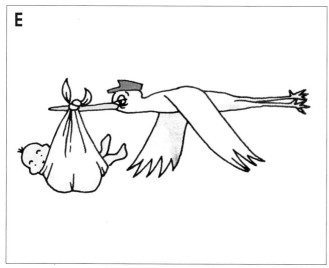

*Does anybody believe this?*

One way in which many religions speak of God is as 'Creator'. We are told that God is the creator of all that exists. It is important that we understand what this means. It doesn't, of course, mean that God actually makes everything that can be found on this earth or elsewhere. We know that cars are 'created' in factories, that paper is 'created' in the paper mill and that babies are 'created' by their parents. Nobody believes that God is busy making all these things and sending them down to earth in some magical way! Rather, what is meant is that without God it would not have been possible for anything to come into existence and that without God nothing that exists could continue to exist.

**G** is an image of the Hindu God Siva. Before we think about it, it's important to understand what we mean by an 'image' of God. No Hindu would believe that this piece of metal was really a God. Nobody would worship the object itself. Rather, worship is given to what the object represents.

If you want to know what you look like, you look in a mirror. There you see your image. It is a reflection of what you are like. In a similar way, an image is a reflection of what the believer thinks God is like. An image says something about the character and qualities that the God is believed to have. By looking at the image the worshipper can concentrate on the God that the image represents.

*Psalm 23 - God likened to a shepherd.*

*Siva - Lord of the Dance.*

Let's apply that to this image of the Hindu God, Siva. Here He is pictured as 'Lord of the Dance'. Everything about Him suggests movement - the position of his arms and legs and his flying hair. Clearly Siva is a God of action. He is, in fact, a God of both creation and destruction.

Destruction is represented by the flames He holds in one hand. In another hand He holds a drum. Siva is the Lord of time. The drum stands for the regular 'beat' of the seasons. The whole universe operates in time with the beat of Siva's drum. Beneath Siva's feet is a small demon. The demon represents evil. Siva is the one who conquers evil.

## CORE ACTIVITIES

There are some religions that do not represent God at all in art. Judaism and Islam are examples. This is because God is believed to be beyond representation. No picture or statue can do justice to what God is really like. A picture can, at best, portray only a part of the complete character and nature of God. So any representation will put improper limits on God.

1 The Bible describes God in many different ways. He is likened, for example, to a King or a Judge. He is sometimes spoken of as a Deliverer or as a Refuge. These may be thought of as images in words. Can you suggest why these images are used?

2 Read Psalm 23 (as printed in **H**). Why does the psalm writer liken God to a Shepherd?

3 Look at the other images of God shown in this unit. What do you think the artists are trying to say about God?

'The Father is God, the Son is God and the Holy Spirit is God. The Father is not the Son, the Son is not the Holy Spirit and the Holy Spirit is not the Father.'

In Christianity you will find many artists' representations of God. Sometimes they depict God as a judge or a king. But, in addition, Christianity has a very special way of understanding the idea of an image of God. If you ask a Christian what God is like you may well get the reply 'Look at Jesus'. Christians believe that once and once only God became a human being - Jesus. The technical word for this is 'incarnation'. The word means 'becoming flesh'. Christians celebrate this event each Christmas. So Jesus is, for Christians, a human image of what God is like, a human mirror or reflection of the character of God.

EXTENSION ACTIVITIES

4 Look at the words of some familiar Christmas carols. Where can you find the idea of Jesus as God in the form of a human being?

5 According to Hindu belief, the God Vishnu took human form as Prince Rama and as Lord Krishna. See what stories you can find about either Rama or Krishna. Find, in particular, the stories that are associated with the Hindu festival of Divali.

# 7. Why do people suffer?

This is a vast question, of course. We can only begin to think about it here. It is the sort of question that many people find themselves asking time and time again throughout their lives and I hope that you will not necessarily be satisfied with the first answers that occur to you.

Some suffering is clearly caused by our own actions, deliberate or otherwise. If we break the law we can expect to suffer some punishment like a fine or imprisonment. If we deliberately touch a live electric wire we can expect at least to be burnt. In these cases people might say that we have got what we deserve. But sometimes human action causes suffering not to ourselves but to other people. If countries go to war they know that many people will be killed and others injured. If you drop an atomic bomb you know that devastation will follow. In these cases, decisions made by national leaders may affect the lives of thousands, perhaps millions, of people and bring suffering to them. This may seem less just, but at least we can still explain why the suffering has happened.

Sometimes suffering is caused by factors outside our control. A violent storm may bring down a tree on a car and kill the driver. A sudden flood or fire may kill many people, or an earthquake bring destruction to a whole town or area. We can say what has caused the suffering but, again, it seems unjust and we cannot help asking why it has happened.

It is when suffering seems unjust that we find ourselves faced with difficult questions to answer. Why should one person who seems to us mean and selfish live to a great age and live a life of wealth and luxury when somebody else who is kind and generous may live in poverty and die young? It doesn't seem fair and we cannot help saying so.

**A**

IN MEMORY OF THE
SIX MILLION VICTIMS
OF NAZI PERSECUTION

ת נ צ ב ה

OUR FATHER. OUR KING. GRANT MERCY
TO US AND TO OUR CHILDREN FOR THE
SAKE OF THOSE WHO WERE SLAIN FOR
THE SANCTIFICATION OF THY HOLY NAME

*They suffered simply because of who they were.*

**B**

*An atom bomb explodes. Why did this happen?*

*Does ageing inevitably bring suffering?*

*Can the suffering being caused here be satisfactorily explained?*

It would not be right to try to summarise here what all the major religions of the world say about suffering. It is too complicated and we could not do justice to even a small part of their teachings. But we can take a brief look at two rather different approaches to the problem of suffering that religions adopt.

The Buddha sought the answer to human suffering.

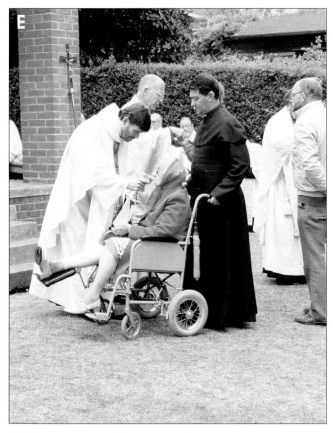

Suffering makes some lose their faith in God. For others, suffering makes faith stronger. Why?

One approach says that in fact the injustice may be more apparent than real. Broadly speaking, this is the approach of the religions that emerged in India - Hinduism, Buddhism and Sikhism. These religions start from the assumption that we have not just one life on earth but many. Our lives may be human or animal or even insect. The type of existence we have is to some extent determined by the life we lived before and our next life will be influenced by the way we live this life. In this way, suffering in this life can be explained at least in part as the results of our thoughts, words and actions in a previous life. In that sense there is a justice at work but you can only see that justice if you look at more than just our present life.

## CORE ACTIVITIES

1 What arguments can you think of for and against each of the following explanations of suffering:
  i   Suffering is a punishment from God.
  ii  Suffering is sent by God to test us.
  iii Suffering is the result of our own foolishness and disobedience.
  iv Suffering is caused by human thoughtlessness.

2 Can you think of any examples of occasions when something good has come out of suffering? Describe one in as much detail as you can.

3 Think of an occasion in your life when you experienced some form of suffering. Can you say what caused that suffering? Do you think that suffering had a purpose?

A rather different approach says that there is suffering in the world because the world as a whole has turned away from God and has rejected Him. Christians, for example, sometimes speak of the world as 'fallen'. By this they mean that the world is no longer as God intended it. Evil has entered the world and has corrupted human nature. People therefore no longer live as God would wish. Some might see suffering as God's punishment for people's disobedience to his laws. But this does not get over the problem of the suffering of people who seem to be good. Why should God punish them? Others, therefore, explain suffering not on an individual but on a larger scale. They suggest that suffering is what inevitably happens when the world as a whole rejects God and all that He wishes and approves. If the world turns its back on what is good, suffering follows. In such a world you must expect injustice.

*The suffering of Jesus is at the heart of Christianity.*

*Can good come from suffering?*

## EXTENSION ACTIVITIES

4 According to Christian belief, God became a human being and suffered an agonising death on a cross. See what you can find out about what Christians believe the purpose of that death was.

5 Invite a Christian priest or layperson into your classroom and find out how the death of Jesus affects that person's understanding of suffering.

6 Invite a representative of some faith other than Christianity into your classroom and ask questions about how that person's understanding of suffering is affected by his or her religious beliefs.

# 8. Worship.

In this unit we shall be exploring what worship is. That will help us understand the part worship plays in the religions of the world.

*Worship in a Progressive Jewish synagogue.*

When, in a rather soppy film, the hero tells the heroine that he worships the very ground on which she stands, what does he really mean? Presumably it's something to do with the fact that he loves her more than anybody else and that he values her more highly than anybody else. This may seem a rather silly example, but it tells us a good deal about the idea of worship.

In its broadest sense, to worship something or somebody is to say that that thing or person is, in your opinion, of great worth or value. You affirm the worth-ship (that's where the word 'worship' comes from) of that thing or person by giving that thing or person your time and attention. In that way you show that it is of value to you. In that broad sense you can worship a football team if that team means more to you than anything else. Similarly we talk about 'idolising' somebody - a pop star, for example - if we turn that person into an idol, an object of worship, by focusing all our thoughts and attention on him or her.

Whether worship of that sort could be described as religious is something you can talk about. But certainly it helps us to understand what is going on in religious acts of worship. In such acts, the worshippers are saying that the God (or Gods) being worshipped is (are) of worth or of value. Indeed, they are usually saying that that God is the thing that is of the greatest worth or value. If you believe that God is the creator and sustainer of all that exists, it is hard to imagine anything that could be greater or more worthy of your worship.

*'Your Worship'.*

Look at **C**. We will think about the second half of this sentence in a later unit. For now it is the first half that is important. At one level the words 'There is no God but Allah' simply mean that no God but Allah exists. He is the only God that there is. But these words have a further meaning for Muslims. They mean that a Muslim must not put anything in the place that Allah should have in the Muslim's life. Allah should be the Muslim's first priority. To give greater priority (ie to attach greater worth) to material possessions like your home or your income, or even to attach greater value to your family than you do to Allah would be to have a 'false God'. Allah alone is to be worshipped, not these other things or people.

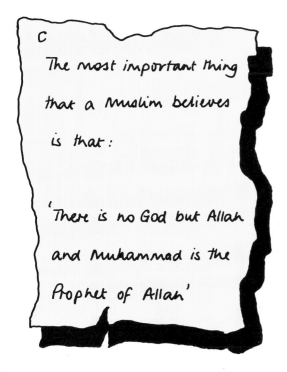

**C**

The most important thing that a Muslim believes is that:

'There is no God but Allah and Muhammad is the Prophet of Allah'

*An expression of submission to the will of Allah.*

For worshippers in other religions, too, God is the only true object of worship. Though they may think of God in different ways, Sikhs, Jews and Christians, like Muslims, worship what they believe to be the one true God. As we have already seen, Hindus offer worship to many Gods and Goddesses, though for many Hindus these are thought of as aspects of one true God.

*Circling the arti lamp before the Gods. The five flames stand for earth, fire, light, water and wind, so all creation joins in the worship.*

When thinking about worship, it is interesting to compare the way religions treat their founders. Hinduism doesn't have a single founder so we can leave Hinduism to one side. For a Jew, however, to worship Abraham would be out of the question. Abraham is thought of as the founder or 'father' of the Jewish people but he is certainly not an object of worship. Similarly Sikhs will not worship Guru Nanak. They respect him greatly and believe that God inspired him. In their worship they sing the hymns Nanak wrote. But they do not worship him. For a Muslim to worship Muhammad would be unthinkable. It would be to worship something other than Allah and that, as we have seen, is contrary to the most basic of Muslim beliefs. It is one thing to respect a founder, something quite different to worship him. For Muslims, the former is permissible, the latter quite unacceptable.

The situation is rather different when we turn to Buddhism and Christianity. In the oldest form of Buddhism the Buddha is looked on as a teacher. He is not divine, nor is he a saviour. He is the person who discovered and taught the basic truths about human life. According to this form of Buddhism,

*Is meditation a form of worship?*

what each individual has to do is to follow the Buddha's teaching and thus discover those truths afresh. In later forms of Buddhism, however, the Buddha came to be thought of more as a divine saviour and so prayer and worship were addressed to him.

*Sikh worship centres around the reading of God's Word.*

In Christianity it is quite acceptable to worship Jesus. This is because Christians (as we have already seen) believe that Jesus was God in human form and that he is alive today and a part of what Christians call 'the Godhead'. According to Christian teaching, the most helpful way to think of God is as three Persons in one God - as God the Father, who created and sustains the universe, as God the Son, Jesus, and as God the Holy Spirit, who guides the church today. Because Jesus is thought of as divine he may be worshipped.

*For some Christians the praise of God matters most in worship ...*

*... for others it is the bread and wine of the Eucharist.*

## CORE ACTIVITIES

1 Be honest! What is the thing or person that matters to you more than anything else?

2 Try to explain in your own words why some founders of religions are worshipped by their followers and others are not.

3 If you believe/believed that God exists/existed, what difference, if any, does/would it make to your life?

### EXTENSION ACTIVITIES

4 What people are addressed as 'Your Worship'? Why is this title used?

5 Find out why Muslims call Muhammad the 'Seal of the prophets'.

# 9. Places of worship.

Though worship could take place anywhere, it is common for people to worship in a building especially designed for the purpose. So, to understand a place of worship like a temple, a synagogue, a church or a mosque, you have to understand the activity that takes place there.

*Wudu, ritual washing, is essential before Muslim prayer. Can you say why?*

Often, of course, there is variety in the way people worship within one religion. That's why, for example, one church may look very different from another. But in general the buildings that belong to each religion have features in common that reflect the way that religion understands worship. Let's look at some examples.

Devout Muslims pray at five times in each day. It's impossible for them always to go to a mosque, so Muslims will frequently pray at home or at their place of work. But the noon prayer on Fridays should be performed in a mosque alongside other Muslims who live in that area.

Often mosques have tall minarets from which somebody called a 'muezzin' can call the faithful to prayer. Many mosques have domes and large open courtyards. But there are really just three things that are absolutely essential in a mosque. One is a large open area where people can pray. It may be under cover or open to the sky. This space is called a 'place of prostration'. Muslim prayer involves frequent prostration (kneeling and then bowing so that the forehead touches the floor) as a sign of humility and respect for the greatness of God. The place of worship must allow for this to happen.

*The mihrab shows the direction for prayer.*

The second 'essential' in a mosque is running water for washing before prayer starts. The exposed parts of the body are rinsed three times. The worshipper is then ready for prayer.

The third 'essential' is something that shows the direction of Mecca in Saudi Arabia. Mecca was the birthplace of Muhammad and, according to Muslim belief, it was there that Abraham built the first building for the worship of the one true God. Consequently all Muslim prayer is performed facing in the direction of Mecca. This direction is called 'qibla' and it is usually shown by a niche in one of the walls of the mosque. If all the worshippers face the niche they know they are facing Mecca.

So purity, humble prostration before Allah and direction are the three essentials in Muslim worship and the place of worship is built so as to cater for these needs.

The dais for the Guru Granth Sahib, focal point in a gurdwara. Why?

The Sikh place of worship is called a gurdwara. 'Guru', here, means God, and 'dwara' means a doorway. So a gurdwara is a 'doorway to God', the place to which you go if you wish to worship God.

One essential thing that must be there is a copy of the Sikh scriptures, the Guru Granth Sahib. This consists largely of hymns of praise to God written by Guru Nanak and subsequent gurus (leaders of the Sikh people) and the singing of these hymns, called kirtan, is the main feature of the worship. During the day the scriptures will be placed on a raised platform in the gurdwara. At night the holy book will rest in a special room set aside for that purpose alone. So, first and foremost, a gurdwara is a building designed to house the scriptures and where people can come together to praise God through the singing of its hymns.

In Britain, many Hindu temples are buildings converted from other uses.

Similarly, of great importance in a synagogue is the 'ark', a cupboard where are kept the scrolls on which the Torah (Jewish Law) is written. The word 'synagogue' means 'a place of assembly' and the synagogue is the place where Jews assemble to hear the Torah read and to study its meaning.

You will not find statues or other images of God in mosques, gurdwaras or synagogues. But in a Hindu temple these are the most notable features. A Hindu visits a temple to make offerings of money, fruit or flowers to the Gods, to pay homage to those Gods and to receive darshan from them. 'Darshan' is hard to translate but it suggests experiencing the Gods' presence and receiving blessing from them.

*The Ark where the Torah scrolls are housed - the most important part of the synagogue.*

Christian places of worship have various names - church, chapel, cathedral and others. They are places where Christians can meet together to praise God through hymns and prayers, to confess their sins and ask for forgiveness, to hear the Bible read and its meaning explained, to give thanks to God for all that God gives and to make their needs and requests known to God. But two features are special to Christian places of worship and each of them reflects a very common household event. The first reflects the simple act of washing, the second, that of having a meal.

The special type of washing that forms a part of Christian worship is called 'baptism'. Sometimes it is performed on adults, sometimes on children, very often on babies. It is understood in different ways by different people. Some Christians see it chiefly as a sign of joining the Christian community, the Christian church; others as a symbol of the washing away of sin and the beginning of a new, spiritually pure life. Others again see it as symbolising a sharing in the death and resurrection of Jesus. However it is understood, there must be a special part of the church where this can take place. In some churches it simply involves the sprinkling of water on a baby's forehead. All that is needed is a form of basin (called a 'font') that can contain sufficient water. In other churches it can involve the person being totally submerged under water. For this a sizeable pool is needed.

*A font with water for the Christian 'washing'.*

Christian worship also centres around a special meal. Almost all Christians take part in this meal from time to time and for many it forms a part of regular Sunday worship. It is known by various names - the Lord's Supper, the Eucharist, the Mass, the Breaking of Bread, the Holy Communion, the Holy Liturgy. Again, its meaning is variously understood, but for all Christians it is at least a way of remembering the last meal Jesus had with his disciples on the evening before his crucifixion. The Gospels record that Jesus blessed bread and wine and distributed them to his friends, the disciples. He likened the bread to his body that would soon be broken and the wine to his blood that would soon be shed. He asked that his followers should repeat this sharing of bread and wine in memory of him. Almost all Christian places of worship have an 'altar' or a 'communion table' that is the focus of this very special aspect of Christian worship.

*An altar - the 'table' for the Christian 'meal'.*

So, in addition to all else, Christian places of worship are built to house the Christians' special washing ceremony, baptism, and meal, the Eucharist or Mass.

## CORE ACTIVITIES

1 Think of the following buildings:
  i  a library
  ii  a house
  iii  a factory
  iv  a sports centre
  How does their design reflect their use?

2 Visit a place of worship near your home. Make some sketch drawings of the inside and the outside. Sketch some of the special furnishings the building may have and try to find out what they are used for.

3 How would you describe the atmosphere of the building you visited? Choose any of the following words that seem appropriate and add any of your own:
calm, cold, confusing, eerie, frightening, peaceful, puzzling, strange, warm, welcoming.

### EXTENSION ACTIVITIES

4 Take some photographs of places of worship near your school. Mount them in a display and attach labels to say who worships there.

5 Find out the meanings of the names Christians give to the meal of bread and wine that they share.

6 Ask representatives of the Baptist Church and the Church of England into your classroom. Ask them to explain their views about baptism.

# 10. Celebration.

We all take part in celebrations. We celebrate the birth of a new baby and, as each year passes, we celebrate that person's birthday. We celebrate engagements and marriages, the passing of examinations, the winning of competitions and all sorts of other things. This unit explores the purpose of celebrations and of religious celebrations in particular.

When we celebrate something what we are saying is that that thing matters to us. We are pleased that a baby has been safely born into the world and that the parents have a new son or daughter. We are pleased that two people we know have decided to marry, that the team we support has won the cup, and so on.

The same is true in the world of religion. When people celebrate a religious festival they are saying that something matters to them.

Children learning about Rama and Sita in order to celebrate Divali.

Like other celebrations, religious celebrations are often happy and sometimes noisy occasions. As with other celebrations, there are often special things to eat and special clothes to wear. There may be special stories to tell or songs to sing. Amidst all the fun of the celebration, however, it is important to understand what is actually being celebrated.

You may have heard of the Hindu festival of Divali. Some of you may celebrate it in your homes. It is particularly associated with lights. Homes are specially lit up throughout the celebrations. At this time Hindus remember the story of Prince Rama and his beautiful wife, Sita. Sita was lured away from Rama while he was in the forest and was taken by the evil demon, Ravana, to the island of Lanka. Rama was distraught, but with the help of the God Hanuman he was able to find Sita and rescue her. Divali celebrates the joy of the return of Rama and Sita to their kingdom.

A wedding is a cause for celebration.

In a sense Divali is about the story of Rama and Sita. But it's also about something else. Rama and Sita represent all that is good. Ravana represents evil. In the story good triumphs over evil, so, at a deeper level, the festival is also about the belief that good is stronger than evil. If you believe that it is certainly something you will want to celebrate.

The use of lights at Divali is rather similar to the use of lights at the Christian festival of Christmas. Streets and shops are full of Christmas lights. In homes there are lights on Christmas trees. Christmas, of course, is the time at which Christians remember the birth of Jesus. Light is often a symbol of happiness, goodness and rejoicing and those ideas are common to Divali and Christmas. For Christians, Christmas is a time to rejoice in the birth of the person they believe to be God in human form come to earth to save people from their sins.

There is another important Christian festival that has a lot in common with Divali. It is, in fact, the most important of all Christian festivals - Easter. Again, many of you will know the story of Easter and some of you may celebrate it at home or in church. The Bible tells us that Jesus was put to death by crucifixion on a Friday. Christians call it Good Friday. But, less than forty-eight hours later, on the Sunday, the Bible claims, he was alive again.

The resurrection of Jesus, if it is true, would be a remarkable enough event in its own right. But for Christians, the more important thing is what the resurrection of Jesus means. Like the story of Rama and Sita, it suggests that good is stronger than evil. Good is represented in the Easter story by God and by life, evil by the cruel death which Jesus suffered. According to the Easter story, God raised Jesus from the dead proving that evil would not have the last word. For Christians, too, Easter points to the idea that death is not the end. There is life with God beyond death. Little wonder that, for Christians, Easter is a time for rejoicing and for happiness!

*Christmas - a time for general celebration, but especially so for Christians.*

Easter tells us something else that is important about celebrations. Though they are usually happy times, there can be sadness in celebration too. Christians celebrate Good Friday as well as Easter Day. They celebrate the death of Jesus as well as his resurrection. This is because both the death and the resurrection of Jesus matter to them. Christians understand the death of Jesus in different ways, but all Christian creeds agree that the death of Jesus was a part of God's way of enabling people's sins to be forgiven. For this reason it is something to be deeply thankful for. For Christians, though Good Friday is in many respects a sombre day, it is nonetheless a day to celebrate.

*Christians speak of 'celebrating' the Eucharist. Can you suggest why?*

*Is this a celebration?*

This sombre side of celebration is something you can talk about as a class. What other examples can you think of? Could remembering the anniversary of the death of a relative be described as a 'celebration'? What about the scene shown in **E**?

It is possible, of course, to celebrate on your own, but as in families, so in religions, most celebrations are community affairs. They are times when people who share common beliefs and values come together to remember events and people or to take part in activities which are important to them.

Perhaps it is not surprising that many celebrations have a particular place for children. If you think for a moment about any festivals - like Divali, Christmas or Easter - that you know about, you will see how true that is. You can see this, too, in the Jewish festival of Purim.

This festival celebrates an event which took place well over two thousand years ago. Haman, a high-ranking official in the service of the King of Persia, was threatening to kill all the Jews who lived in that land, but they were saved by a queen named Esther.

*Purim puppets.*

*What does the Sikh festival of Baisakhi celebrate?*

The book of Esther in the Bible tells the story of this event and it is read in synagogues at this festival. Whenever Haman's name is mentioned, those present, and especially the children, use rattles and boo and hiss so that his name cannot be heard!

You might like to read the story of Esther and find out what part is played by each of the characters in **F**.

Religious celebrations are often fun and entertaining. But for the believer it is the meaning that lies behind the celebration that really matters. The fun and laughter are enjoyable extras!

## EXTENSION ACTIVITIES

4 To explore further the happy side of religious celebration find out what you can about one of the following:
i the Islamic festival of Eid-ul-Fitr
ii the Sikh festival of Baisakhi

5 Find out more about Divali or Purim. Divide your class into two groups for this.

6 To explore further the more sombre side of religious celebration, find out how and why Jews celebrate Yom Kippur.

7 Devise a ceremony designed to celebrate something important to your class.

## CORE ACTIVITIES

1 What things happen in your school or home that are worth celebrating? Make a list.

2 Find a Christian hymn or prayer that is used at Easter time. What does it tell you about the meaning of Easter for Christians?

3 Make a list of things you have celebrated in the last twelve months. In what ways do those things matter to you?

# 11. Knowing and believing.

Beliefs form an important part of every religion. This unit explores some of those beliefs and raises questions about the difference between believing and knowing.

We all know that beliefs form an important part of every religion. If you want to know about a religion, one of the first questions you ask is what the followers of that religion believe. We have already noted, for example, that most religious people believe in the existence of one or more Gods and that they hold beliefs about what God is like. We have seen, too, that they hold different beliefs about the founders of their religions. And there are all sorts of other beliefs.

*How can we know what lies beyond death?*

*How can they know that what they are told is true?*

There are beliefs about the purpose of life. There are beliefs about what happens when we die. There are beliefs about heaven and hell, sin and forgiveness, how we should behave towards each other, or what we should and shouldn't eat or drink. There are beliefs about the creation of the world and about how it will end. Beliefs about angels and spirits and ghosts and demons. Beliefs about holy books and beliefs about prophets. And so we could go on. You will not necessarily find beliefs about all these things in every religion, but each religion has a large number of beliefs that all or most of its followers will accept.

*'He (God) has been made known to men by the grace of the guru.' (Mool Mantra)*

Sometimes the essential beliefs of a religion are gathered together in what we call 'creeds'. The word 'creed' comes from a Latin word 'credo' which means 'I believe'. So a creed is simply a statement of the beliefs of a religion.

'All*ah* alone is God.' *Certainty or belief?*

In an earlier unit we looked at a sentence which sums up the most important of all Muslim beliefs. Another way of expressing that sentence is in **D**.

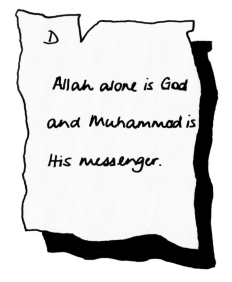

D

Allah alone is God and Muhammad is His messenger.

We discussed the meaning of the first half of the sentence. Look back to page 29 if you have forgotten what we said. The second half of the sentence is of great importance to Muslims too.

Muslims believe that during the course of history Allah has revealed his will and his nature to the world through a number of very special people called 'prophets'. They brought messages from Allah to the people of their day and called people to a correct understanding and a correct worship of Allah. According to Islam, these prophets include many people well known to Jews and Christians like Abraham, Moses, David and Jesus. But Muslims believe that Muhammad was the final and most important prophet. The revelation which he received from Allah and which is now written in the Muslims' holy book, the Qur'an, is, Muslims say, the fullest and the final revelation that Allah will give. So, for Muslims, Muhammad is Allah's final messenger or prophet. He is sometimes called 'the Seal of the prophets'. This is what is meant by the second half of the sentence above.

The most important Buddhist beliefs are summed up in what are called 'the Four Noble Truths'. The Buddha is said to have taught these truths in the first sermon he preached after he had become enlightened.

The first of these 'truths' states that all life is full of suffering and unsatisfactoriness because nothing is permanent. The second states that this suffering arises from our craving for pleasure. The third states that there is a way in which suffering can be stopped. The fourth states that the way to stop suffering is to follow 'the eight-fold path'. This consists of right understanding, right thought, right speech, right action, right means of livelihood, right effort, right mindfulness and right concentration.

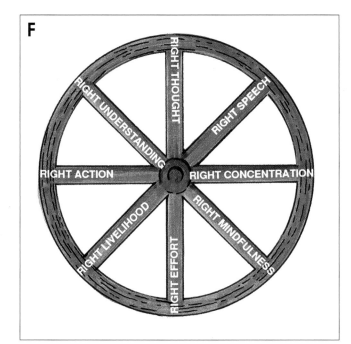

*The Noble Eight-fold Path.*

In Christianity there are two well-known creeds. The shorter is called 'the Apostles' Creed' and it is written in **G**.

G

I believe in God, the Father Almighty, creator of heaven and earth.
I believe in Jesus Christ, his only Son, our Lord. He was conceived by the power of the Holy Spirit and born of the Virgin Mary.
He suffered under Pontius Pilate, was crucified, died and was buried. He descended to the dead. On the third day he rose again. He ascended into heaven, and is seated at the right hand of the Father. He will come again to judge the living and the dead.
I believe in the Holy Spirit, the holy catholic Church, the communion of saints, the forgiveness of sins, the resurrection of the body, and the life everlasting.

*How can the preacher be so sure of what he is saying?*

This unit is called 'Knowing and believing'. So far we have talked only about believing. In our normal speech we use the word 'know' to suggest that we are certain about something or that something can be proved. We use the word 'believe' to suggest that we accept something even though we cannot prove it to be true.

If we apply that distinction to religion we would expect, for example, that a Muslim would say 'I know that the mosque exists' (because you can go out into the street and see it) but 'I believe that Allah exists' (because, as we said in an earlier unit, the existence of God cannot be proved). Similarly we might expect a Christian to say 'I know that there are stories about Jesus in the Bible' but 'I believe that Jesus is the Son of God'.

## CORE ACTIVITIES

1 Do you think it is possible to be certain of anything other than what our five senses tell us? Do our senses ever deceive us? Talk about this in pairs or small groups.

2 Write out the words of the Apostles' Creed. Underline in one colour the words that speak of the three Persons in which Christians think of God. In another, underline the words that relate to Christmas. In a third, underline the words that relate to Good Friday and Easter day.

3 Discuss in pairs or small groups what you think these phrases of the Apostles' Creed mean:
i  holy catholic Church
ii  communion of saints
iii  forgiveness of sins

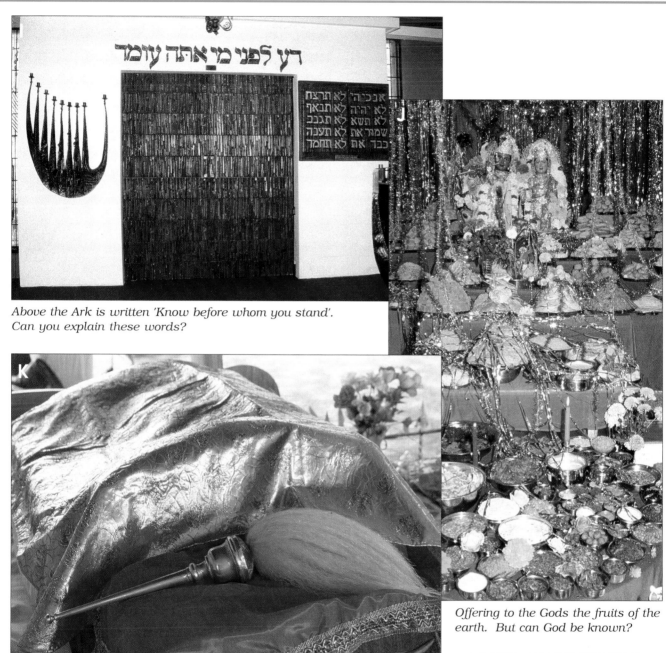

Above the Ark is written 'Know before whom you stand'.
Can you explain these words?

Romala and chauri emphasise the authority of the Sikh scriptures.

Offering to the Gods the fruits of the earth. But can God be known?

To some extent that does happen. The Apostles' Creed begins 'I believe ...'. But it doesn't always happen. Many Christians would claim to know (ie to be certain) that God exists or that Jesus is God's Son. The Muslim statement we have thought about doesn't begin 'I believe ...'. Muslims would say that they know that Allah alone is God. For them it is a statement of fact. There is no uncertainty at all.

How religious people can claim to know things that others would say are matters of belief only is tied up with the question of religious authority, and we shall be thinking about that in the next two units.

4 Find the words of the other frequently used Christian creed, the Nicene Creed. See how many of the ideas contained in the Apostles' Creed you can find in the Nicene creed also.

5 Write your own personal creed. Include the things that you believe (or believe in) most strongly.

# 12. Holy books.

This unit examines one reason why some people claim to know what others might say was 'unknowable'.

If you wanted to find out the answer to a question there are three main things you could do. One is to look the answer up in a book that you believed to be reliable. Another is to ask somebody who you thought was likely to know the answer. The third (if this were possible) is to go and look for yourself. To be extra certain you might try all three! In other words, you could rely on a book, on another person, or on the evidence provided by your own experience. Any one of these could be the 'authority' that you consult. And if two or all three of these authorities supported each other you'd feel extra confident that you had the right answer.

It's rather similar when it comes to matters of religion. One authority that many religious people turn to for answers to their questions is the holy book, the scriptures, of the religion concerned. Some might say that they know (rather than just believe) something because it is contained in their scriptures. Christians, for example, turn to the Bible, Muslims to the Qur'an. Sikhs accept the authority of their holy book, the Guru Granth Sahib. Jews turn to the Torah, the five 'books of Moses' as they are called, the first five books of the Bible.

*Torah scrolls dressed as befits their importance for Jews.*

Hindus have many sacred writings, but a collection known as the Vedas is particularly important. In addition, there are two great epics called the Ramayana and the Mahabharata. The latter contains a section called the Bhagavad Gita (sometimes just 'the Gita' for short) which many Hindus love more than any other scripture. The Buddhist scriptures are in three parts which together are called the 'Tripitaka' (which means the 'three baskets', ie the three collections of writings).

There's one very important thing we must be clear about when we think about the scriptures of the various religions. You mustn't assume that people of all religions treat their scriptures in exactly the same way. Indeed, you cannot assume that all people in one religion have exactly the same beliefs about their scriptures. Let's look at one or two examples.

*The Qur'an, respectfully placed on its stand ready for reading.*

Muslims believe the Qur'an to be the word of Allah exactly as He revealed it to Muhammad through the angel Gabriel. So they accept what is written in the Qur'an. They may need to work out its meaning for today, but they do not question or challenge it. It is 'God's Word'. Some Christians (we sometimes call them 'fundamentalists' or 'literalists') take the same view of the Bible. They believe it to be word for word 'the Word of God', to be believed literally and absolutely. Some Jews (in particular Orthodox Jews) take a similar view of the Torah. To them it is the law exactly as revealed by God to Moses. But you will find other Christians and Jews who take a different view of their scriptures. They believe that the scriptures have authority and that God speaks through them but that they have to be studied in the way you would study other ancient literature.

*Christians speak of the Bible as 'the Word of God'. What do you think they mean?*

Many Christians, for example, would accept that the Bible contains ancient myths and sacred legends as well as history. They would accept too that the history of the Bible has to be checked against the findings of archaeology and that if the two do not agree it isn't necessarily the archaeologists who are wrong. They would accept that some parts of the Bible are more valuable than others and that some have a less than perfect understanding of God. Nonetheless, they would still say that the Bible is a unique book. They would say that it provides more evidence than any other book about what God is like, what God has done and is doing today, and what God wills for the world. They would still say that God communicates with people through the Bible and that it is therefore absolutely essential to the life of Christian individuals and the whole Christian church because it gives guidance on what Christians should believe, how they should behave and how they should worship. It remains a source of authority.

## CORE ACTIVITIES

1 Find out the height of the highest peak in the Rockies, the date of birth of one of your grandparents and your school telephone number. What makes you certain you have got the right answers? In other words, what were your authorities?

2 On what would you expect the following books to be authorities?
   i    a book of recipes
   ii   a road atlas
   iii  a D.I.Y. manual
   iv   the scriptures of a religion

3 Carry out your own researches into the importance of the Qur'an for Muslims, the Torah for Jews or the Guru Granth Sahib for Sikhs. You may like to divide your class into three groups to do this.

EXTENSION ACTIVITIES

4 Explore further the different ways in which Christians view the authority of the Bible. A survey among Christians you know would help or you may be able to persuade a priest or minister of a local church to help you with this.

5 See what stories you can find from the Ramayana or the Mahabharata. Choose one of those stories and turn it into some form of classroom display. Perhaps you could act one out and explain its meaning in a school assembly.

# 13. People and experience.

This unit examines two other sources of authority on which many people base their claims to religious knowledge and certainty.

In all religions you will find people who, because of the study they have done or the degree of knowledge and understanding they are believed to have, are looked upon as religious authorities.

In Buddhism, for example, this is particularly true of the monks. Because of their lives of study and meditation the laity (ie all the people who are not monks) treat them with great respect and honour. They consider them to be higher on the spiritual path

*In what religion is this man a priest?*

and believe that they can acquire religious merit by attending to the monks' needs. They may go to learn from the monks as they listen to them preaching.

*A rabbi instructs Jewish boys in the reading of the Torah.*

In Judaism, the rabbi is the person whose long study of Jewish law makes him an authority respected by the ordinary people. He will be looked upon as the leader of the local Jewish community and will usually lead worship in the synagogue.

In Islam the imam will lead prayer and will deliver the sermon at the Friday noon prayer in the mosque, the prayer when all male Muslims are expected (and females are encouraged) to pray in the mosque rather than elsewhere. The imam is not a priest but a member of the local Islamic community who is respected for his understanding of the Qur'an and for the high quality of the Islamic life he lives.

In Christianity, churches are normally under the care of a priest or minister. It may be a man or a woman (though in some parts of the Christian church it must be a man) who has spent some years studying and training for that job. That person probably has a strong sense of 'vocation' (ie of being called by God to that work). The work of the priest or minister will include the leading of worship, performing baptisms, weddings and funerals, visiting those who are sick or who are in some other form of need, conducting the meetings that are necessary for the running of the church - and much more besides!

*A Christian priest celebrating the Eucharist.*

Because of the role they play in the life of the religious community, all the people we have mentioned - and others besides - may be looked upon as authorities to whom people may turn when they want advice or help on religious questions.

*The granthi reads and cares for the Sikh scriptures.*

*An imam preaching the sermon at the Friday mid-day prayer.*

The third source of authority - personal experience - is suggested by that word 'vocation'. People who are convinced of a calling by God to be a minister or priest may describe that calling in various ways. They may speak of something very dramatic that they can pin down to a particular moment. They may speak rather of a feeling that has grown over a period of time. But however it may come, they are left with an inner conviction that they have been called. They don't need a book or another person to tell them. They 'know' because they feel such a sense of certainty inside themselves.

There are, of course, other religious experiences apart from a calling to the priesthood. Some people claim an experience which they would describe as a 'conversion'. The word 'conversion' means 'turning', so this is an experience which results in such a certainty that they have found religious truth that they turn from one set of beliefs and lifestyle to another. People talk, for example, about being converted to Christianity or Islam.

And there are religious experiences of many other descriptions too. Buddhists speak of the experience of 'enlightenment', an 'awakening' to the truth about the world as it really is which comes about through meditation. The word 'Buddha' means 'enlightened one' and the Buddha is so called because he is said to have been the first to discover these truths (ie the Four Noble Truths which we met in unit 11).

**F**

Meanwhile Saul was still breathing murderous threats against the disciples of the Lord. He went to the High Priest and applied for letters to the synagogues at Damascus authorizing him to arrest anyone he found, men or women, who followed the new way, and to bring them to Jerusalem. While he was still on the road and nearing Damascus, suddenly a light flashed from the sky all around him. He fell to the ground and heard a voice saying,'Saul, Saul, why do you persecute me?' 'Tell me, Lord,' he said, 'who you are.' The voice answered, 'I am Jesus, whom you are persecuting. But get up and go into the city, and you will be told what you have to do.' Meanwhile the men who were travelling with him stood speechless; they heard the voice but could see no one. Saul got up from the ground, but when he opened his eyes he could not see; so they led him by the hand and brought him to Damascus. He was blind for three days, and took no food and drink.

*Acts 9: 1 - 9.*

G

The Buddha is said to have experienced enlightenment.

## CORE ACTIVITIES

1 Suggest some ways in which a religious person might claim to know that God exists.

2 Speak to two people you know who practise a religion and ask them how certain they are about their religious beliefs. Would they claim to 'know' or to 'believe' these things? Talk with them about their reasons for answering as they do.

3 Find an account of somebody's conversion experience. If you cannot find a modern one you can read a very famous one from the early years of Christianity (Acts, chapter 9, verses 1-9) in **F**. How would you account for what the person claims to have experienced? Does knowing about the experience help you understand the person better?

Others may claim an experience of the presence of God. We have already seen how Hindus speak of taking 'darshan' of a God or Goddess. Some people claim to experience the presence of God in worship and particularly in prayer. It may come through a lively style of worship or through the quietness of individual reflection.

*For some, certainty arises directly from experience.*

Christians speak of experiencing the presence of the risen Jesus or of the Holy Spirit. They speak too of experiencing a sense of forgiveness from sin and of being loved by God. And so we could go on for there are many more examples which could be cited. The point that we must take account of is that for many people experiences such as these give a feeling not just of believing but of certainty that they have something that is real. They are therefore willing to speak of 'knowing' the truth that they claim to have discovered.

*I* and *J* both illustrate 'vocations'. In a vocation, who does the calling?

## EXTENSION ACTIVITIES

4 Do some research of your own into the life of a Hindu or Christian priest or a Buddhist monk.

5 Find out what you can about the responsibilities of a granthi.

6 People sometimes speak of being a nurse, a policeman or woman, a teacher, or a solicitor as 'vocations'. What do they mean by that? Do you think it's a good word to use?

# 14. Commitment.

This unit helps us understand what we mean when we say we are committed to something. We see, too, that there are differing degrees of commitment.

Tracey and Richard are brother and sister. They both support the same football club. Tracey goes to all home matches. Her parents gave her a season ticket as a birthday present. She goes to some away matches if she can afford to, but when she can't get to matches she has her radio on and watches television to keep up to date with her team's progress. As soon as she could she joined the official Supporters' Club. Her bedroom is full of match programmes, newspaper cuttings and the like. She has a football signed by all the first team squad. Pictures of the players can be found all over the walls of her bedroom. She can tell you the team's results for the last few years, and for this season's results she can tell you half-time scores, goalscorers, and, in some cases, even the size of the gate.

*Being ordained a Christian priest involves a commitment to Christ and to the church.*

*Commitment to a religion may affect every aspect of your life.*

Richard, on the other hand, has never joined the Supporters' Club. He goes to watch occasionally but often prefers to play soccer with his friends on Saturdays. He never goes to away matches. When he comes home on a Saturday afternoon he gets the score from Tracey. The team hasn't been doing well lately so he says he may be switching support to a more successful club like most of his friends at school.

Tracey and Richard are both supporters. What's different, of course, is their degree of commitment. To Tracey the team is important. To her it means everything. To Richard it's little more than a casual interest. He's involved, but the team doesn't dominate his life as it does Tracey's.

Perhaps we have taken a rather extreme example, but the same sort of thing can happen in the world of religion. To one person the religion is of the utmost importance. For another it has a much lower priority. Tracey and Richard's parents, in fact, are very good examples.

There was a time when Tracey and Richard's father thought seriously about training to be a priest. He had always believed in God. His parents had brought him up in a Christian home. He had a strong feeling that he was being called by God to do a certain job. For some years he thought it was the priesthood or possibly work overseas as a missionary, but in the end he decided that his vocation was to be a doctor. He had become a skilled surgeon and he saw his work of healing as part of the spreading of God's kingdom on earth.

He attended church regularly each week. He would often say that attending the Eucharist was the most important thing he did. He reserved a part of each day - usually first thing in the morning or last thing at night - for prayer and Bible study at home. During the week he attended a study group in the home of other church members. He was actively involved in the work of a charity that his church supported.

*Marriage involves commitment to another person.*

Tracey and Richard's mother was also involved to some extent in the work of the local church. She attended occasionally, particularly at Christmas and Easter and sometimes the Family Services on the first Sunday of each month. She helped with fund-raising events. She didn't go to the mid-week study group. She attended an evening class that day, though she would probably not have gone anyway. She certainly described herself as a Christian but she knew that her husband was more committed than she was. There had been a time when she had felt much as he did and she had thought seriously about being confirmed, but, as the years passed she had become less sure of her faith and so she was now glad that she had decided not to. Certainly she did not feel that she could take part regularly in the Eucharist (the service of Holy Communion) as her husband did. That required a greater level of commitment than she possessed. She preferred to 'take a back seat', as she sometimes put it.

In every religion there are people with differing degrees of commitment. Some are committed to the extent of devoting the whole of their lives to the religion. They may become priests, monks or nuns. Some have been willing to die for their faith. Such people are sometimes spoken of as 'martyrs'. At the other end of the spectrum there are people who belong to a particular culture but who do not really practise the faith at all. A person may, for example, have been born into a Christian or a Muslim or a Sikh home. Or they may have been born in a country or area where that is the dominant religion. They might therefore describe themselves as Christian, Muslim or Sikh but seldom if ever attend a place of worship, say prayers, read the scriptures or do anything else normally associated with practising a religion. And, of course, there are all sorts of positions between these two extremes.

## CORE ACTIVITIES

1 Conduct a survey of the religious practices of as many adults as you can who would describe themselves as belonging to a religion. Find out to what extent they actually practise that religion.

2 Could you claim to practise a religion if you never:
   i attended a place of worship?
   ii said prayers?
   iii read from the scriptures?
   iv tried to help other people?

3 Make a list of any things to which you would say you are committed. How do you show that commitment?

### EXTENSION ACTIVITIES

4 Do some research into the lives of some religious martyrs. Try to include martyrs from more than one religion.

5 Would you describe somebody who dies as the result of a hunger strike for a cause he or she believes in as a martyr? Give your reasons for your answer.

6 Would you describe Jesus as a martyr? Again, give your reasons.

# 15. Belonging.

One way in which we show our commitment to something is by belonging to the appropriate group or organisation. Let's get back to Tracey and Richard whom we met in the last unit.

After his Bar Mitzvah a Jewish boy belongs to the adult Jewish community.

Tracey, you will recall, was a member of the Supporters' Club; Richard wasn't. Their father had shown his commitment to the Christian church by being confirmed; their mother hadn't.

Joining a religious group is a sign of commitment to the beliefs of that religion. You may not necessarily hold all the beliefs, or there may be some things you feel more sure of than others, but a decision which everybody connected with a religion has to make is whether they are sufficiently committed to become full members of that group.

Often there are special ceremonies associated with joining a religious group. Many people look back on these ceremonies as among the most important moments of their lives. Sikhs, for example, who wish to show their personal commitment to the Sikh faith will undergo a ceremony called 'amrit'. They then become members of what is called the 'khalsa' - the community of adult, believing Sikhs . Often this takes place in late teens, but it must be at an age at which the people concerned are capable of making their own decisions and understanding the importance of what they are doing.

A khalsa Sikh.

The word 'khalsa' means 'pure ones'. The amrit ceremony takes its name from the blessed, sweetened water, called amrit, that is used during the ceremony. Five adult Sikhs lead the ceremony. They read from the holy scriptures, the Guru Granth Sahib, while stirring amrit in a large bowl with a sword called a 'khanda'. Those joining the khalsa will drink some of the amrit and have it sprinkled on their eyes and head. Prayers are said and sacred food, called 'karah parshad' is distributed to everybody present.

The use of water in the amrit ceremony is a little reminiscent of Christian baptism which we have already discussed in unit 9. Before you read on, look back at what was said in that earlier unit.

Joining the Christian church is really something that happens in two stages. The first stage usually takes place when you are a baby though it can take place later. In many Christian churches this first stage is called 'baptism' though sometimes the word 'christening' is used instead. This is the time when babies are welcomed into the Christian church and given their Christian names. The parents make promises that, with God's help, they will bring the children up to take part in the life of the church, and godparents (sometimes called sponsors) promise to help the parents bring the children up in the Christian faith. The babies, of course, are too young to make any promises for themselves!

Later in life, when those children have grown up and are perhaps teenagers or adults, they may wish to express their own Christian beliefs and make promises for themselves about being followers of Jesus. If that is so, they will undergo a further ceremony called 'confirmation' through which they become committed, adult members of the Christian church.

*Like confirmation, Believers' Baptism requires a conscious decision.*

In other churches, as we saw in the earlier unit, people are baptised only when they are old enough to make decisions for themselves about what they believe. This type of baptism is therefore called 'believers' baptism'. In these churches there may be a service of dedication when young babies are brought to the church and dedicated to God. This replaces the infant baptism of other denominations.

*Belonging to the sangha, the community of Buddhist monks.*

## CORE ACTIVITIES

1 Read Matthew's Gospel, chapter 3, verses 13-17 and chapter 28, verses 16-20 and then suggest some reasons why baptism is important for Christians.

2 What arguments could you put forward in favour of:
i the baptism of infants?
ii the baptism of adults only?

3 Do you think it's important to have some sort of ceremony that marks the decision to take on a fuller commitment to religious beliefs and practices? Say why you think as you do.

EXTENSION ACTIVITIES

4 Do some research into the significance of the Bar Mitzvah and Bat Mitzvah ceremonies for Jewish boys and girls.

5 Find out what you can about the 'sacred thread ceremony'. It is an important event in the life of many Hindu boys.

6 In what ways is an eighteenth birthday party like the ceremonies we have been thinking about in this unit?

# 16. Responsibility.

Belonging to any group brings responsibility. This unit considers the responsibilities that arise from belonging to some religious groups.

If you are a member of the group we call 'car owners' you have a responsibility to drive with care. If you are a member of the group we call 'citizens of this country' you have a responsibility to keep the law. There are responsibilities associated with belonging to a youth club, a sports team, a family or any other group.

*What responsibilities does Christian belief bring?*

Taking the step of becoming a member of a religious community and committing yourself publicly to its beliefs, practices and values brings certain new responsibilities. More is expected of you than of those who are less committed. Committed Muslims, for example, have five obligations placed upon them. They are listed in **C**.

*Many parents feel a responsibility to bring their children up in their faith and culture.*

C

They should hold the essential belief that "Allah alone is God and Muhammad is His messenger".
They should pray at five set times daily.
They should observe the fast of Ramadan.
They should give a proportion of their wealth to support needy Muslims.
Once during their lifetime they should perform the "Hajj", a pilgrimage to Mecca, the birthplace of the prophet Muhammad.

These five requirements are sometimes called the five 'pillars' of Islam. It's easy to see why. A building is supported by pillars - or some are, at least. Islam is being likened to a building and the five 'pillars' are the five essential beliefs and practices that hold it up.

We have already discussed the first pillar (see pages 29 and 41). The second is a major undertaking. The prayers do not take long to perform but regulating your day so that the five prayer times can be observed calls for a good deal of commitment. It may involve making special arrangements at your place of work or study.

The third pillar is also very demanding. For the whole Islamic month of Ramadan, a committed Muslim will neither eat nor drink during the hours of sunlight. Something we have to remember is that the Islamic year is slightly shorter than the calendar used in this country so the Islamic months move gradually around the solar year. This means that the month of Ramadan can come at any time in the solar year. It may come in winter when it isn't light until about 8 am and is dark again soon after 4 pm. But it may come in the summer when it is getting light at 4 am and isn't really dark until nearly 11 pm. When Ramadan falls in the summer it is a really difficult fast to keep.

*The mosque in Mecca. Every Muslim who is able has a responsibility to visit it as part of the Hajj.*

*Clocks indicate the times for Muslim prayer.*

*There are many consequences of commitment to Islam.*

The fifth pillar may involve the Muslim in saving for many years in order to be able to perform the expensive pilgrimage. For many Muslims it is the high point of their religious life. To keep these five pillars calls for a high level of commitment from each Muslim. For them, religious commitment is not something that can be taken lightly. The responsibilities are very considerable indeed.

A rather different set of requirements is placed upon Sikhs who have become members of the khalsa. They are required to wear five items each of which has symbolic significance. Each begins with the letter K so the five are always referred to as 'the five Ks'. They are:

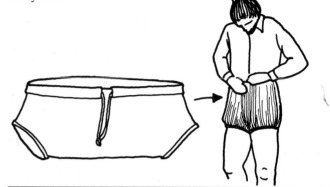

## KACCHA

Kaccha are shorts. In the Punjab in northern India where Sikhism originated they are normal working clothes. In this country they are usually worn as an undergarment. They allow the legs plenty of freedom so they were a convenient style of clothing for a fighting people. They symbolize moral purity.

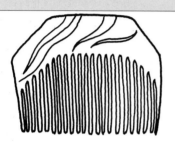

## KHANGA

A khanga is a comb that holds the uncut hair in place. It suggests purity and orderliness.

## KARA

A kara is a thin, steel bracelet which is worn by Sikhs on their right wrists. It symbolizes a number of things. The circle of steel suggests oneness and thus the kara stands for the oneness of God, and because a circle goes on for ever it also symbolises God's eternity. The strong circle of steel also serves as a symbol for the strength and unity of the Sikh people.

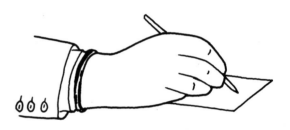

## KIRPAN

A kirpan is a short sword. In their early years, the Sikhs were often a persecuted people and the kirpan reminds them of their past when they literally had to fight for survival. It also symbolizes the obligation, if need be, to fight in defence of their faith. Because the wearing of a sword is illegal in this country (it would count as an offensive weapon) many Sikhs wear a miniature kirpan on a necklace or as a decoration on their khanga.

## KESH

Kesh is uncut hair. Sikh men and women allow their hair to grow and men do not shave their beards. This symbolises acceptance of the way God has created them. It thus suggests humility before God. In India, uncut hair is also seen as a sign of holiness. Holy men called 'sadhus' allow their hair to grow. Together, then, the kesh and the kirpan suggest the idea of a 'soldier saint'.

A Sikh who is a member of the khalsa has the responsibility not only to wear the five Ks but also to take seriously all that they symbolize.

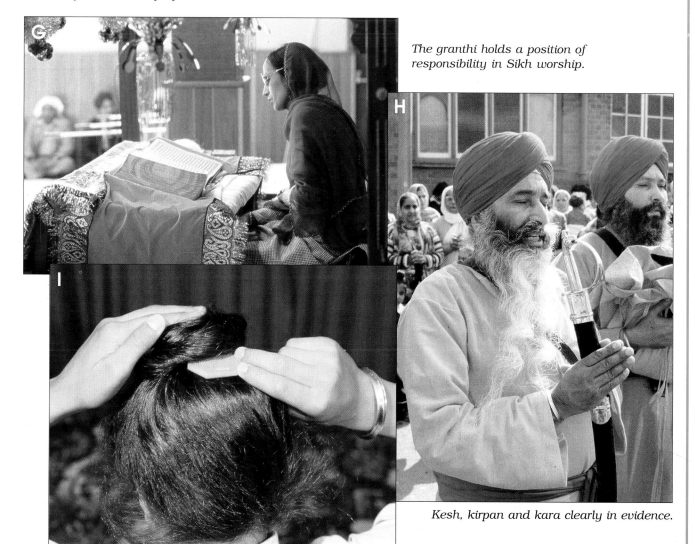

*The granthi holds a position of responsibility in Sikh worship.*

*Positioning the khanga.*

*Kesh, kirpan and kara clearly in evidence.*

## CORE ACTIVITIES

1 Choose three groups to which you belong and list the responsibilities that go with belonging to those groups. What happens if people don't take those responsibilities seriously?

2 Why do you think people are more critical of a priest who gets into trouble with the law than they are of other people? Is it reasonable that people should react like that?

3 Find out when Ramadan starts this year. What will the hours of daylight be? See if you can find out any other rules that apply to Ramadan and which groups of people are exempt from the requirement to fast.

**EXTENSION ACTIVITIES**

4 Find out some more about Islamic prayer. What words are spoken and what actions are performed? Do the actions have any particular significance?

5 Do some research into the reasons why Christians, Hindus or Buddhists go on pilgrimages.

6 Are there any places that have a special significance for you or your family? Could visiting them be described as a 'pilgrimage'?

# 17. Behaviour.

We have seen that commitment to a religion brings many responsibilities. Some of these concern the values those who follow the religion hold. This, in turn, affects their moral code and thus the way they behave towards other people and the rest of the world around them. That's what this unit will consider.

Buddhist laypeople are expected to keep five rules. These are listed in **A**.

**A**
- Not to kill any living creature
- Not to steal
- Not to commit adultery
- Not to tell lies
- Not to drink alcohol or use other intoxicants

A Buddhist monk is expected to keep the five additional rules listed in **B**.

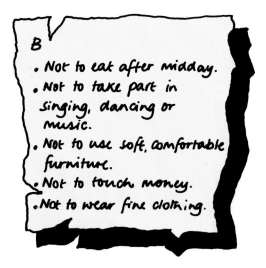

**B**
- Not to eat after midday.
- Not to take part in singing, dancing or music.
- Not to use soft, comfortable furniture.
- Not to touch money.
- Not to wear fine clothing.

Do Core Activity 1 before you read any further.

*A Buddhist monk keeps ten precepts.*

The Buddhist rules may remind you a little of another set of rules called the 'Ten Commandments' which are of great importance to Jews and Christians because they are found in the scriptures they share. They are found in the Book of Exodus, chapter 20, verses 3-17. They are summarised in **D**.

**D**
- To worship nothing other than the one true God.
- Not to make, nor bow down before any images or idols.
- Not to misuse God's name.
- To keep the Sabbath day holy.
- To respect parents.
- Not to commit murder.
- Not to commit adultery.
- Not to steal.
- Not to testify falsely against anybody.
- Not to covet anybody's wife or possessions.

What similarities can you see between these sets of rules? What are the main differences?

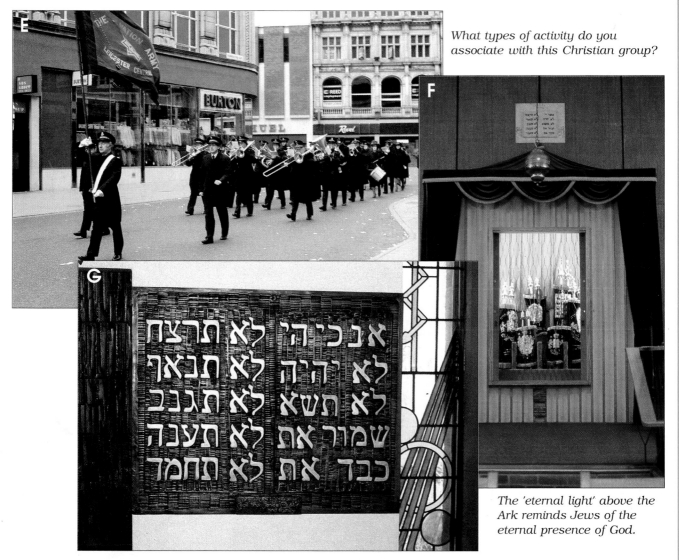

*What types of activity do you associate with this Christian group?*

*The 'eternal light' above the Ark reminds Jews of the eternal presence of God.*

*The opening words of each of the Ten Commandments in Hebrew.*

According to the New Testament, Jesus was one day asked what the most important commandment found in the whole of the Torah (Jewish Law) was. He replied, in fact, by quoting two passages from the Torah. The first is in Deuteronomy, chapter 6, verse 5. You can read it in **H**.

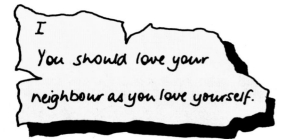

H

You should love God with all your heart, with all your soul and with all your strength.

The second is in Leviticus, chapter 19, verse 18. You can read it in **I**.

*Who is my neighbour?*

I

You should love your neighbour as you love yourself.

You can read Jesus' full reply in Matthew's Gospel, chapter 22, verses 34-40 in **L**. For Christians, the answer that Jesus gave has been the guiding rule concerning their conduct towards other people. It can be summed up as 'love for other people arising out of love for God'.

*Religious belief affects family life.*

L

Hearing that he had silenced the Sadducees, the Pharisees met together; and one of their number tested him with this question: 'Master, which is the greatest commandment in the Law?' He answered,' "Love the Lord your God with all your heart, with all your soul, with all your mind." That is the greatest commandment. It comes first. The second is like it: "Love your neighbour as yourself." Everything in the Law and the prophets hangs on these two commandments.'

*Matthew 22: 34 - 40.*

In Hinduism there is a very important idea called 'ahimsa'. That word is usually translated as 'non-violence'. It implies that a Hindu should not kill or even harm any living creature. It results in Hindus having a great respect for all forms of life, human and animal, and great respect for nature in general. In consequence, many Hindus are vegetarians. Hindus believe that within all living creatures there is something which is everlasting. It is called the 'atman'. It is sometimes translated by the English word 'soul'. The atman is what passes from one existence to the next when one earthly life is over. Because all living creatures contain this eternal element they are, in a sense, holy, and merit respect.

*Respect for the Divine is at the heart of Hinduism.*

*Gandhi has been described as the most important religious figure of the twentieth century.*

## CORE ACTIVITIES

1 Take each of the ten Buddhist rules in turn and try to explain what its purpose might be. You may need to talk about this in pairs or small groups. Why do you think the monks have the five additional rules?

2 Which of the Ten Commandments relate to the Jew's or Christian's attitude towards God and which relate to their attitudes towards other people?

3 Leviticus 19:18 speaks of loving your neighbour as yourself. Discuss the idea of loving yourself. What do you think it means? It sounds selfish! Can loving yourself be a good thing? Can you love other people if you do not love yourself?

EXTENSION ACTIVITIES

4 Do some research into the life of Mahatma Gandhi. In what ways was the idea of ahimsa important for him?

5 Is ahimsa a practical idea? Is it possible to live life that way? What differences would it make to your life if you were to try?

6 Can you think of an occasion when it might be right not to tell the truth?

# 18. Resources.

Here are some books that may help your researches:

## General books about religion

Bailey J.R. **RELIGION IN LIFE Series** - *Schofield and Sims*
Bennett O. **EXPLORING RELIGION Series** - *Bell and Hyman*
Brown A., Rankin J. and Wood A. **RELIGIONS** - *Longman*
Collinson C. and Miller C. **BELIEVERS** - *Edward Arnold*
Mayled J. **RELIGIOUS TOPICS Series** - *Wayland*

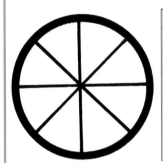

## Books about Buddhism

Bancroft A. **THE BUDDHIST WORLD** - *Macdonald*
Ling T. **BUDDHISM** - *Ward Lock*
Naylor D. and Smith A. **THE BUDDHA - A JOURNEY** - *Macmillan*
Snelling J. **BUDDHIST FESTIVALS** - *Wayland*
Thompson M.R. **BUDDHIST TEACHING AND PRACTICE** - *Edward Arnold*

## Books about Christianity

Brown A. **CHRISTIAN COMMUNITIES** - *Lutterworth*
Brown A. **THE CHRISTIAN WORLD** - *Macdonald*
Curtis P. **CHRISTIANITY** - *Lutterworth*
Curtis P. **EXPLORING THE BIBLE** - *Lutterworth*
Curtis P. **THE CHRISTIANS' BOOK** - *Lutterworth*
Rankin J. **CHRISTIAN WORSHIP** - *Lutterworth*
Rankin J. **THE EUCHARIST** - *Lutterworth*
Shannon T. **JESUS** - *Lutterworth*
Shannon T. **CHRISTMAS AND EASTER** -*Lutterworth*
Thompson J. **THE CHRISTIAN FAITH AND ITS SYMBOLS** - *Edward Arnold*
Thompson J. **CHRISTIAN BELIEF AND PRACTICE** - *Edward Arnold*
Thorley S. **CHRISTIANITY IN WORDS AND PICTURES** - *RMEP*

**Books about Hinduism**

Bahree P. **THE HINDU WORLD** - *Macdonald*
Cole W.O. **MEETING HINDUISM** - *Longman*
Ewan J. **UNDERSTANDING YOUR HINDU NEIGHBOUR** - *Lutterworth*
Mitter S. **HINDU FESTIVALS** - *Wayland*
Sharma D. **HINDU BELIEF AND PRACTICE** - *Edward Arnold*

**Books about Islam**

Ahsan M.M. **MUSLIM FESTIVALS** - *Wayland*
Iqbal M. and M. **UNDERSTANDING YOUR MUSLIM NEIGHBOUR** - *Lutterworth*
Protheroe R. and Meherali R. **VISITING A MOSQUE** - *Lutterworth*
Thompson J. **ISLAMIC BELIEF AND PRACTICE** - *Edward Arnold*
Thorley S. **ISLAM IN WORDS AND PICTURES** - *RMEP*

**Books about Judaism**

Charing D. **THE JEWISH WORLD** - *Macdonald*
Charing D. **VISITING A SYNAGOGUE** - *Lutterworth*
Domnitz M. **UNDERSTANDING YOUR JEWISH NEIGHBOUR** - *Lutterworth*
Thompson J. **JEWISH BELIEF AND PRACTICE** - *Edward Arnold*
Thorley S. **JUDAISM IN WORDS AND PICTURES** - *RMEP*
Turner R. **JEWISH FESTIVALS** - *Wayland*

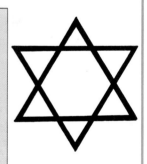

**Books about Sikhism**

Babraa K. **VISITING A SIKH TEMPLE** - *Lutterworth*
Cole W.O. **THINKING ABOUT SIKHISM** - *Lutterworth*
Kapoor S.S. **SIKH FESTIVALS** - *Wayland*
Sambhi P.S. **UNDERSTANDING YOUR SIKH NEIGHBOUR** - *Lutterworth*
Singh D. and Smith A. **THE SIKH WORLD** - *Macdonald*

# Acknowledgements.

## PHOTOGRAPHS

All photographs taken and supplied by Philip Emmett except:

5C, 6C, 6D, 31I, 40B, 40C, 46B, 47C, 47E, 49J, 52B, 54A, 54B, 57G, 57H, 60J Roger Bradley
12B, 27H  The British Red Cross Society
13D  Science Photo Library
14E  Collections - Anthea Sieveking
16A  Susan Sergeant
16B  The Royal Commission on the Historical Monuments of England
18E  Natural Science Photographs
24B  Greenpeace
25D  The Royal Society for the Prevention of Accidents
28A, 52A  Jewish Education Bureau
28B  Norwich City Council
36B, 49I  Folens Collection
38E  The Royal British Legion
60K  Judith Threadgold
61H  Popperfoto

Our thanks to all concerned for permission to reproduce photographs.

## THANKS ARE ALSO DUE TO

Oxford and Cambridge University Presses, for permission to reproduce extracts from the *New English Bible*, second edition © 1970:

22H  Psalm 23
48F  Acts 9: 1 - 9
60L  Matthew 22: 34 - 40

Rev. Cannon R.P. Protheroe, Director of Education, Diocese of Bristol for his helpful suggestions on revising the text.

The Hengrave Hall Community, Bury St. Edmunds, Suffolk, for their kind permission to use 16B.

## ILLUSTRATORS

Denby Designs

Cover design:
Tanglewood Graphics,
Broadway House,
The Broadway,
London SW19
Tel: 081 543 3048

Cover illustration:
Abacus Publicity Limited,
Extension Road,
Caxton Hill,
Hertford SG13 7LY
Tel: 0992 589077

Folens Publishers have made every effort to contact copyright holders but this has not always been possible.  If any have been overlooked we will be pleased to make any necessary arrangements.